SRA OPEN COURT READING

Marge's Barge

A Division of The McGraw-Hill Companies

Columbus, Ohio

www.sra4kids.com

SRA/McGraw-Hill

A Division of The McGraw·Hill Companies

Copyright © 2002 by SRA/McGraw-Hill.

All rights reserved. Except as permitted under the United States Copyright Act, no part of this publication may be reproduced or distributed in any form or by any means, or stored in a database or retrieval system, without prior written permission from the publisher.

Printed in the United States of America.

Send all inquiries to:
SRA/McGraw-Hill
8787 Orion Place
Columbus, OH 43240-4027

ISBN 0-07-569738-6
 2 3 4 5 6 7 8 9 DBH 05 04 03 02

Marge lived on the water.
Marge was in charge of a barge.

Marge's barge was large.
Marge called her barge
"General Danger."

The water rocked the barge.
The rocking was gentle.

Marge had a pal. His name was Gage. Gage suggested Marge change the name of the barge.

"I think General Danger is a strange name," said Gage.
"What can I name it?" asked Marge.

Gage felt "Gem" was a good name.
Now Marge's barge is called Gem.